ARCHITECTURE & DESIGN LIBRARY

COUNTRY VICTORIAN

ARCHITECTURE & DESIGN LIBRARY

COUNTRY VICTORIAN

Ellen M. Plante

FRIEDMAN/FAIRFAX
PUBLISHERS

A FRIEDMAN/FAIRFAX BOOK

© 1997 by Michael Friedman Publishing Group, Inc.

Library of Congress Cataloging-in-Publication Data

Plante, Ellen M.
        Country Victorian / by Ellen M. Plante.
            p.   cm.
        "The architecture & design library."
        Includes index.
        ISBN 1-56799-453-9
        1. Victoriana in interior decoration.   2. Decoration and ornament,
Rustic.   3. Country homes.   I. Title.
        NK2115.5.V53P56   1997
        747.2'048--DC21   97-7239
                                                                                CIP

Editor: Francine Hornberger
Art Director: Kevin Ullrich
Layout Design: Meredith Miller
Photography Editor: Wendy Missan
Production Manager: Camille Lee

Color separations by Colourscan Overseas Co Pte Ltd.
Printed in Hong Kong by Midas Printing Ltd.

3   5   7   9   10   8   6   2

For bulk purchases and special sales, please contact:
Friedman/Fairfax Publishers
Attention: Sales Department
15 West 26th Street
New York, New York 10010
212/685-6610   FAX 212/685-1307

Visit our website:
http://www.metrobooks.com

For my family, and with special thanks to my editor, Francine Hornberger.

C o n t e n t s

INTRODUCTION

Having the best of both worlds: the country Victorian interior is just that, and so much more. By combining two distinct styles—country and Victorian—beautiful rooms are created that blend simplicity with a touch of romance and a dose of subtle, restrained elegance.

Born of the nineteenth-century passion for homey comfort and solid good looks, today's Victorian revival in interior design, and most especially the country Victorian look, allows us to blend select touches of Victoriana with simplified country living, so appealing in our fast-paced, modern world.

The history of country Victorian decorating can be traced back more than a century to the Victorians' penchant for country life and the great outdoors. In the 1863 architectural plan book *Holly's Country Seats*, author and architect Henry Hudson Holly noted, "It seems scarcely necessary at this day to bring forward any formal arguments in favor of country life. It has been the favorite theme of philosophers and poets in all times. Its pure and elevating influences, its comfortable ease, its simplicity and cheapness [economically speaking], have been urged again and again in grave essays and pleasant pastoral and bucolic meditations."

How did the Victorians decorate their country or manor homes? And what of the middle-class farmhouse, or small homes or "cottages" in remote villages and rural settings? Removed from the hustle-bustle and strict formality of city life, country dwellers adopted decorative schemes that were at once comfortable, inviting, and scaled-down compared to the more ornate and elaborate homes of city folk. Interiors were lighter, architectural embellishment was generally kept to a minimum (exceptions of course included Victorian seaside homes and the large manor houses of the well-to-do), and furnishings were often a medley of styles—perhaps cast-offs from a city home or beloved pieces slightly worn but cherished nonetheless.

OPPOSITE: *Recalling an old English country cottage, this vibrant setting is flavored with subtle touches of Victoriana. The first impression may be one of wonderful, vibrant color, but upon closer inspection, homey touches grace this inviting dining area. A tablecloth dresses the table in traditional Victorian fashion and Windsor chairs provide ample seating. In contrast, exposed wood beams on the walls and ceiling conjure a rustic country feel. A soft window treatment of white draperies brightens the blue walls, and a comfortable, upholstered easy chair—complete with pillow—is the perfect spot to enjoy a cup of tea.*

Regardless of where they lived, Victorians in general were concerned to a greater or lesser degree with interior design and noted the introduction and demise of various styles throughout the nineteenth century. Popular etiquette placed significant importance on properly outfitting one's dwelling as both a retreat from the harsh realities of an industrializing world and as a measure of success and social standing.

Due to the machine age and mass production, items once afforded only by the wealthy were suddenly within reach of all. Railroads and mail-order catalogs meant that even in the most remote corners of the country a woman could be fashionable and yet selective in decorating her country home with functional, beautiful pottery pieces, colored glass dishware, choice wallpapers, and then-popular furnishings. Practicality was foremost; excessive fussiness had no place in the country home. A wood floor in the semiformal manor house might be strewn with oriental rugs while cozy needlepoint or rag rugs were put to use in the informal farmhouse setting.

Although the 1980s Victorian Revival in interior design cast country Victorian as a substyle of Victorian decorating, the past decade has seen this substyle move to center stage and blossom into a strong, viable approach to home fashion. Specialty magazines target the country Victorian enthusiast and cottage industries are turning out accessories, furnishings, and textiles with the country Victorian interior in mind. Noted furniture manufacturers have created lines offering the comfort of country and the appealing good looks of Victoriana while mail-order curtains can be bought in everything from chintz to lace.

ABOVE: *Country Victorian enthusiasts are generally avid collectors. Grouping like items can have dramatic results as this wall devoted to cherished items clearly conveys. A potpourri of nature-inspired prints, vintage plates, and artistic tiles are hung in a pleasing arrangement that becomes an instant focal point. A sofa created from an old iron bed is lavishly outfitted with pillows sporting decorative designs and handiwork. And while less can be more, this photo happily depicts the theory that abundance can also be beautiful.*

OPPOSITE: *A more formal country Victorian living room features a typical ottoman serving as a coffee table and a gilded over-mantel mirror. A casual couch and chair, as well as a basket of dried flowers at the fireside, are country touches.*

The popularity of country Victorian style stems in part from its versatility. It can be semiformal or informal—whatever is suitable to your tastes and the needs of your lifestyle. Furniture slipcovers, room arrangements, and decorative accessories can easily be changed to evoke either mood.

Today's country Victorian interior calls for soft, light colors on walls or old-time country hues such as reds, blues, greens, or deep shades of yellow. Any number of wall treatments can be used to achieve the desired casual effect—for example, paint or a wallpaper pattern sporting a miniprint, stripes, or a lovely floral motif. Beadboard wainscoting painted white or a shade to blend with the rest of the room is a decorative effect that strongly conveys country Victorian spirit.

Wood floors are simple yet elegant when polished or with a time-worn appearance. The addition of an area rug such as an old Turkey carpet or needlepoint throw can create a focal point or help define a specific space.

Furnishings in a country Victorian setting should be complementary but clearly need not match. Wicker, warm golden oak pieces, and roomy upholstered chairs, sofas, and ottomans are ideal choices for the country Victorian interior and can be used in tandem with splendid results—a rustic Adirondack chair or table is reminiscent of Victorian mountain retreats while the warm patina on an old painted cupboard would make the perfect backdrop for cherished collectibles.

Architectural embellishments need not be ornate to add character to a room. Substantial crown, window, and door moldings sans carved designs can be striking. Fireplace mantels of warm wood can be more inviting than their marble counterparts and even something as small as an old porcelain doorknob adds a notable touch of charm.

Fresh flowers and plants, along with carefully chosen accessories such as pillows, throws, books, pottery, and vintage collectibles, enhance the semiformal or informal atmosphere of the country Victorian home and personalize each and every room.

"Country Victorian" and "collections" seem to go hand in hand. Scout flea markets and antiques shows for time-worn fabrics and textiles, architectural artifacts, favorite antiques, and what have you. Keep in mind that country Victorian is not primitive pieces, folk art, or wooden bowls—all of which are categorically considered "country"—but nature-inspired objects such as shell-covered boxes or framed, floral prints along with the machine-made objects that filled the homes of long ago.

On the pages that follow, you will find inspired ideas for designing country Victorian rooms—from the welcoming entryway and the comfortable parlor to the inviting dining room, the romantic bedroom, and the spirited kitchen and bath. Country Victorian design can bring to your living space all the timeless appeal that makes a house a truly special home.

OPPOSITE: *A coordinated look is achieved through the use of wallpaper and a creative window treatment. A miniprint and florals in autumn tones create an eye-catching background. The window valance has been designed to match the wallpaper border. An old iron bed plays up color with a striped pillow and comforter standing ready for chilly nights. An antique dresser is home to a rock collection and bouquet of flowers while favorite prints and paintings grace slanted walls.*

CHAPTER ONE

WARM, WELCOMING ENTRYWAYS

Throughout the nineteenth century, charming country houses were built in small towns and villages all across North America. Rural areas, too, were dotted with manor houses, and resort locations were of course popular for second homes or "cottages." The various architectural styles in vogue during the Victorian era resulted in a landscape resplendent with subtle Greek Revival–style farmhouses, eye-catching Gothic Revival–style cottages, Italianate villas, and numerous vernacular interpretations of those styles that came and went during the later years of the gilded age.

Façades were dressed with color, and natural materials such as timber, brick, and stone were used in building the country Victorian home. Harmony with nature was a keypoint to architectural detailing and the main entry was all-important in conveying a hearty "welcome." A small portico or a substantial front porch provided a gateway to the comfy interior beyond the front door. A casual attention to detail was—and still is—as obvious outdoors as in.

Regardless of architectural styling, typical nineteenth-century houses included an entryway or foyer which not only set the tone for the homes' interior decor but also served as a functional space designed to receive coats, hats, boots, umbrellas, and of course visitors.

Depending upon the size of the home, the entryway was either small but serviceable or large and grand. Its architectural embellish-ments and background mirrored that of the other rooms in the home, whether formal or informal.

Furnishings specifically designed for the entryway included hall trees made of wood or metal that incorporated a mirror, hooks for hats and coats, and even a seat (with a lift-top providing storage under-neath) into a singular design. In addition, wall-hung mirrors flanked by hooks were popular in small spaces for parking hats or bonnets. A sturdy table was often found in the foyer along with a side chair for guests waiting to be received.

In outfitting today's country Victorian entryway, there are a wide range of choices to be made in regard to background and furnishings. Bright colors are ideal in evoking country spirit; pastel shades can

OPPOSITE: *A playful country Victorian spirit is conveyed by this inviting seaside cottage. An abundance of architectural trim, or "gingerbread," is a hallmark of the gilded age, and is nicely accented by the light blue exterior of the home and its stand-out white and hunter green trim. Hanging baskets and a plant stand filled with flowers on the porch add the perfect touch to a setting that speaks of carefree days and casual style.*

infuse the setting with a hint of Victorian romanticism. A checkered ceramic tile floor or a wood floor accessorized with an eye-catching needlepoint rug will convey a more casual style. Simple crown moldings, wallpaper borders, or stenciling can clearly define the space between walls and ceiling. A front door can be painted a complementary color and dressed up with a lovely porcelain, brass, or glass doorknob.

A vintage or reproduction oak hall tree or even a cast-iron tree painted white are right at home in the country Victorian entryway, as is a brass or wood freestanding coatrack. If space is at a premium, consider brass or porcelain wall hooks mounted on a painted or gleaming wood plank board. A small blanket chest or vintage trunk can be used here for storage or even as a tabletop. A painted bench or old church pew are but two ideas for casual seating.

Last, but by no means least, accessorize your country Victorian entryway with an informal display of flowers or baskets. An old crock can be given new life as an umbrella stand; a wreath of dried flowers can dress up the door. A brass hanging fixture or a ceiling fixture with an attractive frosted glass or colored glass shade will warmly light the way indoors. The possibilities for evoking a relaxed spirit are endless.

ABOVE: *Color has dramatic impact on this covered entryway while the rope-turned columns and ornamented pediment are a striking visual effect. The front door is painted to match the porch and the decorative iron fence continues the color theme, demonstrating how small touches can impart country Victorian style.*

OPPOSITE: *Set among beautiful gardens or scenery, the country Victorian home offers a safe haven from the outside world. Mountains and a lake provide a breathtaking backdrop for this casual country manor house. The country Victorian spirit reigns supreme; exterior embellishments are kept to a minimum and a simple hedgerow and rose bushes complement the warm patina of the old stone façade.*

A B O V E : *The quintessential country Victorian "cottage," this circa 1840s Gothic Revival–style house flaunts a beautiful soft rose exterior, a welcoming entry protected by an ornamented veranda, and pointed dormers with decorative bargeboard and finials that reach toward the heavens. Reminiscent of European medieval architecture, the Gothic Revival style was popularized in North America by architect Andrew Jackson Downing during the mid-nineteenth century.*

O P P O S I T E : *This charming Victorian home happily coexists with its natural surroundings by using earth tones in the palette of the porch and the time-worn beauty of a brick driveway. The deep green, orange, yellow, and gold trim work is a wonderful example of harmonizing with nature while the flower bed contributes show-stopping accent colors. Attention to detail is apparent in the carefully painted porch and its restrained ornamentation.*

LEFT: *This spacious entryway is the perfect example of how less can indeed be more. A vintage hanging fixture casts soft lighting and a warm glow, and a minimalist approach to furnishings and accessories allows the elaborate doorway to take center stage. The slender sidelights and dramatic fanlight create an impressive architectural embellishment that calls for little else. A handsome oriental rug contributes a dash of pattern and design while allowing the beauty of the hardwood floor to shine through, achieving subtle country Victorian ambience.*

RIGHT: *Country Victorian goes high style in this elegant entry, dressed with a notable wall treatment. The tripartite walls (walls divided into three distinct sections—dado, field, and frieze) are reminiscent of the Victorian gilded age and are held in check by the simplicity of a select few furnishings and accessories. Even the ceiling has been adorned. The unassuming light fixture balances the ornate view overhead.*

RIGHT: *A touch of romance lingers in this inviting country Victorian entryway. The colors featured in the front door's art glass window are repeated in the mauve color of the walls and the cobalt blue glass vase holding fresh flowers. A small bookcase and plant stand hold pride of place here and the fringed portiere repeats the color scheme, adding a notable artistic touch.*

ABOVE: *Sometimes sneaking in through the back door reveals the most wonderful surprise—in this case, a homey kitchen with stone floor and timbered walls with a charming bench for sliding boots off and on. A handsome clock was de rigueur in many Victorian entryways, and the one pictured here is a beautiful example. A green hutch provides space for cherished objects.*

OPPOSITE: *Semiformal country Victorian elegance is everywhere apparent in this appealing entryway. Combining all the elements of the style—from furnishings and accessories to the backdrop—this foyer calls upon old-world charm and classic good looks to welcome guests. The fanlight above the door adds architectural interest as well as providing natural light in the foyer. A soft, muted color on the walls plays host to important artwork. Handsome and sturdy case pieces provide a convenient spot for select items and a notable bench with throw pillows offers a comfy, inviting seat. An oriental rug is a delightful accent to the floor, and serves as a focal point in this well-appointed and charming setting.*

LEFT: *Manor house charm is the message conveyed in this inviting country Victorian foyer. The elegance of the brass hanging fixture and ornate mirror are complemented by subtle touches of greenery and flowers in bloom. A handsome floor runner leads the way down the hall where visitors pass a tabletop figurine sporting a straw-brimmed hat. A simple touch such as this keeps the setting from becoming a bit too serious and reinforces a more relaxed theme.*

ABOVE: *This Victorian vignette has a country flair with its potpourri of casual floral arrangements and select collectibles. A beautiful vintage table is ideal for holding books and pottery and the casual country-blue rag rug plays nicely against the Victorian-inspired wallpaper. To complete this setting, a lace portiere adds a delicate touch of texture.*

A B O V E : *At first glance the beauty of the art glass windows in the doorway captures all the attention, but it is the use of pattern and design that visually pulls you into this entryway. The specially designed carpet and floral wallpaper combine to create a casual warmth that serves as the perfect backdrop for choice artwork, cherished objects, and a practical yet handsome clock. Country Victorian spirit is further enhanced by the addition of a cane-back chair, a hall table, and a lovely marble-top case piece that not only provides storage but also a convenient place to drop mail and keys.*

A B O V E : *A semiformal spirit sets the tone in this well-appointed entry. The ceiling medallion above the hanging light fixture, handsome cornice, and fringed window dressing add a distinct touch of Victoriana while the warmth of the wood floor outfitted with an oriental rug and personal accessories atop the wood furnishings point to the comforts of country life. Extra details, such as the umbrella stand, make the perfect first impression.*

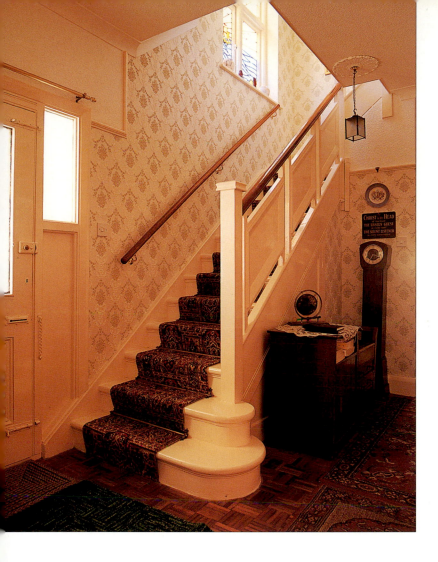

LEFT: *Soft colors in this entryway are a tribute to country Victorian style. A delicate wallpaper is accented by the mellow cream used on the front door and staircase. The parquet floor, oriental stair runner, and small but lovely ceiling medallion add just the right touch of formality. Furnishings and accessories have been chosen with care to enhance the warm, welcoming spirit of this setting.*

RIGHT: *A sturdy pram stands ready for a stroll in this foyer complete with an old-fashioned chandelier and warm, plankwood flooring. Favorite artwork and photos share the spotlight with a table that's home to a collection of bowls. Baskets casually stacked underneath add country charm while the arched entryway and white wainscot on the walls contribute Victorian flair.*

CHAPTER TWO

THE COZY, COMFORTABLE PARLOR

Well-to-do Victorians may have called it the drawing room, but for the nineteenth-century middle class, it was the parlor. This parlor, or living room (as it later came to be known), was a beehive of family and social activity and was without a doubt the best room in the house. Regardless of whether they were urbanites or rural dwellers, the Victorians lavished careful attention on the parlor to create a cozy, comfortable setting where family could join together for an evening's entertainment (perhaps songs around the piano) or the mistress of the house could converse with the minister's wife over a cup of tea.

The old-time parlor was a carefully orchestrated blend of furnishings and accessories that complemented the room's decor. In the country Victorian setting, interior design was simpler than, yet every bit as lovely as, the design of other rooms.

In today's country Victorian parlor or living room, architectural details such as a wood-beamed ceiling, a simple ceiling medallion, notable windows, and a polished wainscot can have as much impact and appeal as gilded trims and carved moldings.

Using wallpaper in a beautiful cabbage rose pattern is an all-time favorite for evoking a more romantic mood in a country Victorian setting. Special paint techniques such as ragging or sponging walls can be used to create a striking country appeal. Painting the ceiling to match the walls or in a shade just a bit lighter is also a wonderful decorative effect. Plain white walls can be enhanced by painting trim and borders in a vibrant accent color.

Visual images of a country Victorian parlor call to mind a wood floor with an oriental, needlepoint, or rag rug as a focal point. While this is an appropriate and popular option, wall-to-wall carpeting can also anchor the room and even add artistic merit if bedecked with a lovely floral or foliage motif.

Among the multitude of furnishings handcrafted or factory-produced during the last century, several styles or forms are especially at home in a relaxed country Victorian setting. Using new or

OPPOSITE: *A medley of patterns is featured in this parlor with smashing results. Checks and florals in the furnishings and draperies complement one another while the playful diamond-patterned wallpaper reigns supreme throughout the room. The fireplace is decked out with artistic tiles and subtle wall sconces put the spotlight on the symmetrical display of objects atop the white mantel. A charming upholstered ottoman adds extra comfort. The parlor table has plenty of room for treats, like afternoon tea, as well as treasures.*

reproduction pieces such as a comfy, upholstered sofa, a chair with matching ottoman, and perhaps a wicker armchair or two will make for an inviting room. Furniture can be arranged symmetrically (along walls) for a semiformal air or in more intimate groupings for a casual, relaxed effect. Rather than using lavish brocades and velvets, consider upholstery fabrics such as chintz (especially small floral prints), damask, gingham, tapestry, or ticking, which are available in a multitude of colors and patterns. Florals and stripes are a mainstay of country Victorian style, but for something a bit more bold, how about a striking tartan plaid?

A scrubbed pine coffee table, a warm cherry wood bookcase, an old oak desk, a bamboo whatnot shelf, a painted hanging wall cupboard, or perhaps a wicker plant stand are just a few ideas for adding accent pieces from the past.

In the parlor, windows can be dressed up or down. Shutters and lace panels are popular but so too are delicate swags, jabots, and decorative valances. A lovely curtain panel can be hung and then pulled to one side, held in place by a simple rosette.

Personalize your country Victorian parlor or living room with sumptuous wool throws for a chilly evening and plump pillows that invite curling up. Scatter small ottomans (upholstered and skirted) about the room to continue the comfort theme. Lighting in the form of tabletop lamps and wall sconces will imbue the room with spirit. Look for lamps with beautiful pottery bases and fabric shades or vintage replicas with colored glass globes that are reminiscent of Victorian times. Family photos atop the mantel, fresh flowers in a pottery vase, and books stacked on a table or chair or even beside the sofa turn your parlor into a more formal a "living room." As always, collections on display create a focal point and a one-of-a-kind personal touch.

ABOVE: *With all the charm of a nineteenth-century cottage, this parlor takes country Victorian decorating to heart. The nickel-plated parlor stove not only provides heat but adds a touch of flashiness to the room. A hand-painted glass shade on the ceiling fixture is adorned with delicate glass prisms for added elegance. Plank flooring is outfitted with a beautiful needlepoint rug, and a Victorian center table, complete with marble top, holds a treasured family book on top of a lace doily. The wallpaper is accented with a favorite country hue—mustard. Beyond the parlor, the bedroom continues the subdued color theme.*

ABOVE: *A handsome wallpaper and carved cornice make a dramatic impact in this parlor with romantic overtones. An eclectic mix of upholstered and hardwood furnishings creates a relaxed setting and calls upon two all-time favorite patterns—stripes and florals. Careful attention to detail pulls the room together, including nature-inspired wall hangings, the needlepoint area rug, books stacked upon the coffee table, and scattered floral arrangements. A tiny footstool stands ready in front of the hearth where the mantel pays tribute to the owner's favorite objects.*

ABOVE: *A hallmark of Victorian decorating, this tabletop vignette of treasured objects is infused with a casual air thanks to the floral-trimmed teal table cover and nature-inspired wicker furnishings seen in the background. By juxtaposing a glorious gilt-framed photo with the simple lines of the art pottery pieces, the fanciful and the sublime have been combined for a modern-day interpretation of country Victorian style.*

OPPOSITE: *While bold colors can be beautiful, this parlor shows that combining various shades of white, cream, and beige also achieves striking results. The dark-wood tones in the ceiling beams are repeated in the wood furnishings but the upholstered pieces, walls, and carpeting brighten the setting by playing with soft and subtle hues. Semiformal country Victorian elegance is further enhanced with a notable window treatment combining drapes with a scalloped valance. Finishing touches such as framed artwork, flowers, candlesticks, and a collection of ornate wooden boxes make this house an inviting home.*

LEFT: *The quintessential bright-red painted Victorian library takes on country charm through a collection of carved animals lined up on the mantel top. A slipcovered sofa and armchair offer classic, casual appeal and pillows galore invite curling up with a book. The handsome mirror above the fireplace and decorative, carved cornice hint at old-world charm in this room that pays honor to both the classic and the contemporary.*

RIGHT: *The ottoman is crucial piece of Victorian furniture. This modern-day interpretation of country Victorian style puts this fabric topped ottoman to work as a coffee table making the perfect spot to keep small comforts associated with "home." The living room is further enhanced by the gallerylike collection of paintings and select collectibles on display.*

ABOVE: *Reminiscent of a robber baron's country estate, this impressive parlor is all that country Victorian style has to offer. The rugged timbered ceiling and crisp white walls provide the backdrop to sumptuous Victorian furnishings and an abundance of accessories. From the floral fabric and decorative braiding on the corner couch to the red velvet chair with fringe and the button-tufted velvet trunk, Victoriana is conveyed at every turn. Beautiful needlepoint rugs, artwork, and treasured objects make this an unforgettable room.*

LEFT: *Extended living areas such as outdoor porches or conservatories pay homage to Mother Nature and are especially fitting for a country Victorian decor. In this space, a profusion of plants and flowers mingles with a bamboo table set for tea. A cushioned bench and chair are accompanied by a vintage upholstered easy chair complete with padded arms and an abundance of Victorian tassles. An oriental rug adds old-fashioned style underfoot and a Gothic arched window complete with colored art glass panes recalls nineteenth-century style.*

ABOVE: *Soft and subtle decorative effects create instant country Victorian charm in this extended living space. The fireplace has been updated with a coat of white paint; a burst of flowers in an old crock steals the spotlight when the hearth's not in use. Easy-care slipcovers in delicate shades dress the two loveseats, and walls washed with a warm color unite the kitchen, dining, and living areas. Accessories, including baskets and plates hung on to walls, books, flowers, and candlesticks, add a personal note and suggest a relaxed, inviting style.*

ABOVE : *Modern-day interpretations of Victorian style offer a broad range of appeal. The casual but classy decorating scheme here introduces a laid-back approach to the Victorian Revival in interior design. The comfy nineteenth-century fainting couch offers the perfect spot to relax and enjoy the view. A beautiful oriental rug defines the conversation area, and the simplicity of the country pine mantel is juxtaposed with an ornate over-mantel mirror complete with shelves for bric-a-brac. The room provides a wealth of Victorian details: Victorian architectural prints hang on the wall, dried floral arrangements are scattered throughout, a vintage jug sits in front of the hearth, and an art glass motif has been placed in the center window pane. The end result is a wonderful rendition of country Victorian style.*

OPPOSITE : *The very essence of country Victorian style, this parlor boasts a medley of elegant touches and casual whimsy. The ornate chandelier and mirror blend beautifully with comfy upholstered furnishings. Accessories such as an ottoman serving double-duty as a coffee table, a hearth-side basket filled with firewood, a collection of candlesticks atop the mantel, and sumptuous throw pillows create a most inviting effect. With furnishings informally arranged around the fireplace, this is an ideal spot for relaxing with guests or curling up with a book.*

LEFT: *Who says white can't be dramatic? Clean, crisp walls provide the ideal backdrop in a room where select furnishings command center stage. The epitome of country Victorian decor, this fabulous parlor makes use of vintage, upholstered furnishings and an attractive wooden trunk in the seating area. A light-filtering art glass window, notable door frames, and a beautiful fireplace with a substantial over-mantel mirror and shelves add architectural flair. Oriental rugs enhance the beauty of the hardwood floor and casual objects such as the basket of dried flowers atop the mirror introduce surefire country charm.*

LEFT: *Country colors steal the scene in this parlor with old-world charm. Salmon walls and a blue hearth are accented with a hand-painted panel depicting a country scene below the mantel and a Victorian-inspired wallpaper border near the ceiling. Candlelight makes the gilt-framed mirror shimmer and casts warm shadows about the room. The rich patina of the wooden chair and table pay tribute to years gone by and the entire room speaks of solid comfort with favorite collectibles close at hand and treasured artwork casually displayed.*

ABOVE: *A decorative cornice is used as an elegant trim for warm red walls in this admirable parlor. Victorian touches and country accents unite with marvelous results—a fringed, fabric-shaded chandelier illuminates a table with a plaid throw. The footstool beside the hearth and the tabletop lampshade at the far right continue the use of plaid. A handsome upholstered armchair is outfitted with comfy throw pillows, and small oriental rugs are scattered about the muted beige carpet for comfort as well as to add color. Wood furnishings and casual accessories such as baskets, candlesticks, and flowers complete the style of the room.*

ABOVE: *Blue, long a favorite "country" color, mixes wonderfully with distinct Victorian touches such as the colorfully detailed screen behind the sofa, the golden-oak fireplace mantel, and the art glass hanging light fixture in this parlor. Casual and comfy, a profusion of accessories such as throw pillows, books, family photos, floral arrangements, and a one-of-a-kind coffee table enhance the appeal of the room.*

ABOVE: *Smaller spaces can be made dramatic through the use of color. Cornflower blue walls are accented by plush burgundy draperies and carpet. An oriental rug brings out both striking shades. The gallerylike assembly of framed photos above the sofa also adds color, as well as balance and texture. Fresh flowers are always at home in a country Victorian setting and here a blue and white pitcher, coordinated with other pieces of pottery, makes the perfect vase.*

CHAPTER THREE
INVITING DINING ROOMS

Given the fact that most socializing and entertaining was done in the home during the nineteenth century, the majority of houses were designed and constructed with a separate dining room. Whether large or small, certain furnishings were necessary. The design of the room itself often echoed the parlor—with colors used in reverse.

Tables and chairs, sideboards, and china cabinets were often sold in suites during the Victorian era. Accessories ranged from ornate sterling silver and crystal in the homes of the well-to-do to silver-plated utensils, pottery, and cheerful colored glass in the typical rural home.

Creating a country Victorian theme in today's dining room, whether it's a separate space or an area adjacent to the living room, provides numerous possibilities in regard to decoration and furnishings. For example, walls can be wood paneled for a rustic effect or treated to a striped wallpaper for a touch of casual elegance. White paint provides a crisp background in which furniture and fabrics take center stage while a medium hue in a green, blue, or rose will unify the design scheme.

A wood floor in the dining room calls to mind the old-fashioned country keeping room and can be enhanced with a carefully chosen area rug in typical Victorian fashion, perhaps an oriental rug or Turkey carpet. Wall-to-wall carpeting can visually blend a living and dining area into one large and inviting space.

In outfitting the country Victorian dining room, dark woods will contribute a more formal effect, so look to a sturdy oak or a warm cherry wood to complement your more casual setting. Round, oval, and rectangular tables can be accompanied by matching Windsor chairs or attractive pressed-back chairs. Chairs in various styles can be used about the table to provide seating as long as they look similar to

OPPOSITE: *Joined together in a picture-perfect setting, casual and formal decorative elements achieve smashing results. An ornate crystal chandelier proudly resides over the table while unadorned wall sconces flank the mirror over the hearth. An elaborate cornice mingles with a small-print wallpaper and dark green paint on dining room doors. The marble fireplace mantel is accessorized with small bouquets of dried flowers and a simple clay pot filled with fresh blooms stands beside the hearth. The fine china has been used to set an elegant table while a casual arrangement of greens serves as a fitting centerpiece.*

each other. Matching chintz chair pads or needlepoint seat cushions can help coordinate your customized approach to gathering around the table. Chairs with cane seats are another excellent choice for the country Victorian dining room.

To provide ample space for dishware and collectibles, consider a vintage or reproduction sideboard, which can be plain and simple or a bit more substantial with a notable marble top. A china cabinet, too, can not only contribute much needed storage space but allow you to create lovely displays of cherished items.

Wicker is always a welcome addition to the country Victorian dining room. A wicker table and chairs painted white add a lightness to the room with their woven patterns and nature-inspired texture. Perhaps a singular piece, such as a wicker planter filled to overflowing, is all that's called for to enhance a cozy and intimate space.

Windows can become a focal point in a semiformal setting when treated to a handsome swag or valance over light and airy curtain panels. For a more restrained look, painted shutters or cafe curtains are as functional as they are attractive.

Wildflowers gathered in a lovely pottery vase or basket make a wonderful centerpiece for the table, and accessories such as brass candlesticks, white ironstone dishware, or colored glass can be used to create striking table settings. Chintz-themed china (china bedecked with small, lovely floral patterns) will add a romantic note when given pride of place in a china cupboard or hung on the wall. Artwork, such as a serene still life or vintage lithographs, can further enhance the old-time spirit of the room.

In lighting the country Victorian dining room, an old-fashioned hanging fixture of brass with glass globes is perfect for above the table, while wall sconces can be strategically placed to provide soft accent lighting.

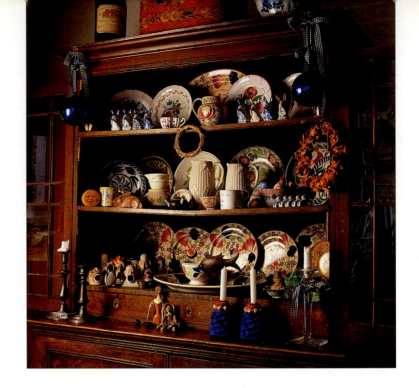

ABOVE: *Step-back cupboards or an old hutch are ideal for displaying collectibles in the country Victorian dining room. In this cupboard, glass-paned doors have been left open to better reveal the potpourri of treasures inside. Antique dishware, pitchers, a collection of whimsical figurines, and bunnies are among the owners' passions.*

OPPOSITE: *By using the natural materials popular during the Victorian age, this enchanting dining area sets a casual, inviting tone. A ceramic tile floor, wooden cupboards, and a timbered ceiling combine to create the perfect backdrop for country Victorian furnishings and accessories. The rectangular dining table is joined by benches with charming blue and white cushions. The blue and white theme continues on the walls and in the plates hung for display. A shelf above the counter is ideal for a vintage enameled canister set. Floral curtains and a beautiful hanging fixture above the table contribute a very Victorian flair to this old-fashioned country setting.*

ABOVE: *A casual country Victorian decorating scheme pervades every corner of this inviting dining room. Late-nineteenth-century charm is apparent in the rectangular oak table, the handsome area rug, and the stylized wallpaper. Sheer café curtains lend a romantic touch, as does the Victorian privacy screen that decorates the corner. A simple but lovely table setting of white china is made complete with a colorful centerpiece of fresh flowers. Ever popular with the Victorians, a botanical painting on the wall echoes the soft, floral theme found in the wallpaper.*

RIGHT: *A Victorian backdrop complete with decorative fretwork, art glass windows, beautiful crimson walls, and a lovely patterned carpet is tempered by the modern-day country influence of minimal accessories on display and the simple beauty of a gleaming wood table. Semiformal and sophisticated is the tone of this dining room.*

LEFT: *Proving that the right accessories can make a world of difference, this dining room is made all the more striking by an eye-catching table setting complete with a colorful, decorative tablecloth. The aged, faded-blue-paneled walls are complemented by rich blue shiny upholstery on the chairs. The blue oyster dishes also play upon the color scheme. A collection of pottery pieces are displayed in the built-in cupboard beside the hearth and as an elegant final touch, a vintage brass lighting fixture is set up to cast a warm glow upon the table.*

BELOW: *Understated and elegant, this intimate dining room is warmed by yellow walls and a country-inspired chandelier. Candlelight, a Victorian favorite in the dining room, is also used on the table and in the wall sconce. Upholstered chairs invite lingering over a meal and conversation. The private view outside the window is enhanced with simple draperies. A lush fern in a classical urn imparts Victorian style and spirit.*

ABOVE: *Architectural embellishment has been called into play in this dining room with stunning results. Deep-set windows, a curved wall in the kitchen area, and an ornate cornice at the ceiling contribute to the semiformal appeal. A vintage chest of drawers (reminiscent of something once found in a general store) serves as a center island and has an architectural flair all its own. The vast expanse of wall has been treated to a sponge-painted effect for dramatic impact. Open racks display crisp, white dishware. The table in the foreground is appropriate to the manor house theme but is lightened by using a mixture of chairs. The impressive chair at the head of the table is true to Victorian charm: its ornate quality bespeaks opulence.*

ABOVE: *Country and Victorian styles truly come together in this dining room. A formal, marble-top Renaissance Revival–style sideboard commands attention with simple country touches. Blending various furniture styles can impart a casual tone, and as seen here, understated chairs with cane seats soften the ornate overtones of the sideboard. In addition, a floral rug and intricately patterned wallpaper provide a romantic, country-style backdrop.*

ABOVE: *The dining area in this kitchen blends Victorian romance with country charm. Enchanting window treatments set off the wainscoted and wallpapered walls, giving the room a polished look. The table is accompanied by casual upholstered chairs and a wing chair that suits the head of the table. Other details include a fringed area rug that defines the eating area and a carefully arranged table setting, which includes a centerpiece of fruit and matching topiaries. Finally, the beautiful cupboard in the background sports matching candlestick lamps that contribute accent lighting to the lovely collection of dishware.*

ABOVE: *This eclectic country Victorian dining room is a visual feast. Patterns and color set the tone as a deep red hue on the walls coordinates with chair cushions, scatter rugs, the wallpaper border, and curtain tiebacks. The wallpaper border is used to create a chair-rail effect behind the table. A sizable country clock balances the more ornate touches in the room, such as the elaborate over-mantel mirror above the red hearth.*

ABOVE: *This cozy dining space affords an attractive view of the outdoors and makes full use of available space. Casual cottage ambience is created by combining a harvest table with a medley of chairs and by tucking a tall chest against a back wall. Books, plates, candlesticks, and decorative wall hangings contribute to the eclectic decor.*

RIGHT: *A stucco wall provides an eye-catching backdrop for collections displayed to perfection in this country Victorian dining room. The unusual vaulted, tounge-in-groove paneled ceiling is a dramatic feature of the room.*

RIGHT: *This homey dining area is a wonderful, if unconventional, example of country Victorian style. Some of the subtle elements of country include an aged harvest table, spirited blue cabinets, kitchen collectibles on display, and hearts lined up atop the mantel. A Victorian highchair stands ready for young diners and enhances the space with a flair of Victoriana.*

LEFT: *The formality of this dining room comes from the tripartite wall treatment and elegant Victorian accessories like the white over-mantel mirror and fabric-shaded hanging fixture. Simple country touches such as the unadorned bucket bench and its collection of dishes, pottery, compotes, and bowls give the room a more casual feel. Country flavor is further enhanced by the assortment of chairs at the table and the use of a natural basket beside the hearth for firewood.*

OPPOSITE: *Country Victorian decorating can range from the casual to the formal. A handsome table and chairs is accompanied here by an equally striking sideboard. A Victorian folding screen used strictly for decoration occupies a corner, and the nature-inspired motif of the gilt-framed painting presides over the room. An oriental rug and floral draperies with a scalloped and fringed valance add an elegant touch to this manor house setting.*

ABOVE: *The formal dining room was often reserved for special occasions and entertaining during the nineteenth century, so many families ate their meals near the warmth of the kitchen cookstove—a trend that continues today. This sizable farmhouse or cottage kitchen easily accommodates a massive wooden table and colorful ladderback chairs. Light blue walls are decked out with favorite dishware on display and the all-important kitchen clock. Throw rugs add pattern and comfort underfoot. Even a vintage piano with a pedestal stool is allotted space in this casual country Victorian setting. A vintage stove adds old-fashioned charm and makes this dining area all the more inviting.*

ABOVE: *With all the charm of a mid-nineteenth-century farmhouse, this kitchen with dining area conveys classic country Victorian style. A massive Victorian cookstove sits next to the hearth and a wooden dry sink proves that functional items can also be beautiful. A vintage drop-leaf table sits upon a braided rug. A crisp, white pantry used for storage can be seen through the kitchen doorway. Select accessories, such as a simple shelf outfitted with a Victorian clock and kerosene lamps, a simple yellow bowl atop the table, and an old jug beside the sink convey the country Victorian theme.*

CHAPTER FOUR

ROMANTIC BEDROOMS

Regardless of whether it was a spacious room on the second floor, a hideaway tucked under the eaves, or a cozy attic retreat, the Victorian bedroom—like today's bedroom—was a personal sanctuary as well as a necessary spot for sleep.

Matching chamber or bedroom suites often outfitted the nineteenth-century boudoir, especially in the urban homes of the well-to-do, but it was not unusual to find a medley of pieces pressed into service in country homes. In addition, nineteenth-century cottage furniture, affordable and appealing with painted finishes and hand-decorated designs, was a mainstay in many a rural bedroom. Beds, dressers, chests of drawers, night tables, washstands, dressing tables, and privacy screens for dressing were among the popular furnishings in bedrooms a century ago. The room itself—often decorated with subtle, floral wallpapers and soft rugs—was a welcome retreat from the hubbub of daily life.

Ornamentation was generally kept to a minimum in the bedroom, especially toward the end of the nineteenth century when sanitary measures began to call for exposed wood floors and metal beds that could be kept sparkling clean and germ-free. White iron or brass beds were—and still are—a hallmark of the Victorian-inspired bedroom.

In keeping with the country Victorian theme, search out examples (vintage or reproduction) that are simple, yet lovely, and not overly embellished with curlicues and ornate trim. Or, if you prefer the warmth and patina of wood, look to an eye-catching four-poster bed. Oak, cherry, or pine are ideal in the country Victorian bedroom.

A pine dresser, a painted wardrobe, a wicker dressing table, or a matching suite of golden oak pieces with delicate carved designs will recall the romantic spirit of the past and blend easily with an attractive mix of other furnishings. If space permits, a comfy upholstered chair or wicker chaise longue makes a perfect spot to relax.

Walls in the romantic country Victorian bedroom can be painted or papered, or a painted wainscot can be used to add a touch of architectural flair. While pastel shades are a longtime favorite in this

OPPOSITE: *An antique French bed commands attention in this charming bedroom. A ribbon-and-floral patterned wallpaper combined with wall-to-wall carpeting and a cascade of draperies looped back with a braided cord create a feeling of elegance. An attractive upholstered chair adds comfort and the full-length oval mirror is as functional as it is decorative. A softly lit bedside table keeps family photos close by to encourage sweet dreams.*

setting, bolder country colors such as red or deep blue can make for a striking background. A stencil design on the ceiling adds a dose of country charm.

Wood floors with or without area rugs and painted floors with a protective finish are wonderful choices for an inviting bedroom. Wall-to-wall carpeting, however, will provide added warmth and can be easily layered with throw rugs for further decoration.

Window dressings such as matchstick blinds, bamboo shades, shutters, lace panels, or colorful chintz curtains are all wonderful choices for the country Victorian bedroom, offering variety in texture and design. When curtains are coordinated to match a stunning floral bedspread, an especially romantic appeal is created.

A generous supply of sumptuous pillows piled high on your bed, quilts, bed ruffles, favorite linens, and lace can all be used to inspire romance. In contrast, simple country practicality can be achieved by limiting bed accessories to a favorite pillow and quilt—less can be more.

A bedside table (which can be something out of the ordinary like an old trunk or small bench) complete with a brass lamp for reading and an inviting stack of books or magazines clearly conveys a spirit of solid comfort. Place cherished objects such as family photos or select collectibles (vintage dresser sets, talcum powder tins) atop the dresser to create an attractive vignette. Flowers, baskets, perhaps a collection of Victorian bonnets—these are just a few examples of everyday objects that become important elements of the decor in a country Victorian bedroom.

ABOVE: *With the arrival of the twentieth century, interior design and furnishings became simpler. This country Victorian bedroom recalls the early 1900s with the plain lines of an Arts and Crafts–inspired bed, but dresses it up with an eye-catching drape at the headboard. Assorted masks and prints adorn the walls, reminiscent of a fussier time. The wallpaper border coordinates with the cozy comforter and curtains, and stacks of pillows add a touch of romance.*

RIGHT: *Crocheted trim on the canopy of this ornately carved bed is the crowning glory in this country Victorian bedroom. The pale pink walls and darker pink ceiling create an ideal backdrop for the burgundy comforter and dust ruffle, and are a typical Victorian color combination. Wall-to-wall carpeting is dressed in a "layered" effect with throw rugs. Floral curtains are looped back to allow natural light to seep in. The regal qualities of the bed are juxtaposed with simple pine chests of drawers and an antique dome-top trunk wearing signs of original paint.*

OPPOSITE: *A luxurious canopied bed takes center stage in this handsome retreat. Color and select accessories play up the manor house ambience while pattern and texture recall the Victorian era. A dome-top trunk resides at the foot of the bed and an armchair is draped with an inviting velvet throw. The intricately carved, tall formal mirror reflects the architectural beauty of the fireplace across the room.*

RIGHT, TOP: *Sleeping quarters during the nineteenth century were decidedly feminine or masculine. This handsome, masculine bedroom is complete with a twin-size brass bed along with plaids, throws, striped wallpaper, and a beautifully designed bed cover. An ornate cornice and window treatment give the room polish while playfulness comes through in the toys and collections on display.*

RIGHT, BOTTOM: *Victorian gilt-framed paintings and deep blue walls give this bedroom a "rich" look; the oriental rug contributes pattern and color. Country estate charm is echoed in the handsome desk and chair. The otherwise ornate daybed takes on a semiformal tone when draped with cotton and linen.*

LEFT: *Perhaps summer vacations spent in a cottage by the sea inspired this cozy, inviting bedroom. A beautiful floral wallpaper adds a touch of romance in this setting. Despite the twin iron beds, a simple oak dresser, and small desk, there is enough space for comfortable armchairs to be positioned to take in the view. A vintage wicker table provides an ideal spot for books, flowers, or teacups. The cushioned window seat with soft throw pillows is a delightful spot from which to enjoy the charming simplicity of the room.*

ABOVE: *This bedroom with daybed is accessorized with piles of lacy pillows and a looped-back curtain that can be drawn in front of the bed for privacy. A bedside table draped with lace tablecloths, a dresser sporting a lacy dresser scarf, and a lace window dressing that matches the bed curtain tie the room together and create a beckoning sanctuary. Stenciling adds an artistic and playful touch to the walls. An old-fashioned country sampler and a dried floral wreath complete this wonderful country Victorian boudoir.*

LEFT: *What a perfect sanctuary is this bedroom with a view. Country Victorian style is clearly evident in the furnishings chosen to outfit this converted attic space. A wooden bed—complete with a patchwork quilt—and a vintage wicker rocker are all that's called for in this small space, which is cleverly maximized by the built-in shelves and drawers. The sloped ceiling also adds spaciousness, and the windows, artwork in themselves, are left bare to take full advantage of the stunning vista.*

ABOVE: *A brass rod has been incorporated into the headboard of this bed; a playful striped valance at the window is suspended from a matching rod. Two wicker baskets at the foot of the bed are used for storing personal items. The quilt rack behind the beautifully upholstered armchair can be used to store bedding and is also decorative. Lighthearted prints are lined up above the bed and an ottoman serves as a spot to enjoy tea and the morning paper. Casual sisal carpeting defines the seating area and natural wood beams outline the room.*

ABOVE: *Unmistakable country Victorian style is found in this casual retreat. Twin iron beds painted white are dressed with matching patchwork spreads and polka-dot pillows. A typical color of both country and Victorian tastes, blue is used throughout the decor. Matching curtains and the bouquet of fresh flowers on the windowsill reinforce the comforting color and pattern scheme, proof positive of the appeal of simplicity.*

ABOVE: *Sometimes a singular furnishing can convey a strong sense of style in itself. Here a magnificent iron bed, lavishly decorated with floral medallions and intricate scrollwork, has Victoriana written all over it. A bedspread of white lace accompanied by playful country-style pillows is all the adornment needed to complement this fancy furnishing. In keeping with the spirit of nineteenth-century style, ephemera has been framed and serves as artwork.*

LEFT, TOP: *Romantic influence and country charm join together in this cozy bedroom. Blue walls encourage rest and relaxation while the white frieze at the top recalls late-nineteenth-century interior design. A beautiful Victorian iron bed—complete with curlicue designs—becomes a focal point and shares space with a vintage oak dresser and storage trunk. Subtle details such as the fabric lampshade, the straw hat resting on the bedpost, a floral area rug, and dried flowers gathered in a basket reinforce the decorating scheme.*

LEFT, BOTTOM: *This beguiling little girl's bedroom makes full use of lovely floral prints to achieve a country Victorian look. Several patterns blend nicely together, and delicate touches such as the lace valance and the wallpaper border would please any young lady. The red Victorian dollhouse is a focal point in this adorable space, both for its bold color and unmistakable design.*

OPPOSITE: *Country and Victorian complement each other beautifully in this feminine bedroom. The ornately sculpted painted iron bed and decopaged lamp instill the space with a sense of Victoriana while floral wallpaper and curtains grace the room with country charm.*

A B O V E : *This quintessential country Victorian bedroom has all the romance and appeal of a secluded bed and breakfast. A handsome four-poster bed is placed against a floral backdrop. A country-style striped rug in the same palette has been added for good measure. Homey comforts such as the casual armchair adorned with knitted afghan and plump pillow and the sleek wooden stool with brass handle to reach the high bed are both functional and decorative. A bedside table displays a charming Victorian vignette while the simple grapevine wreath at the head of the bed typifies a more casual approach to the style.*

RIGHT: *This under-the-eaves bedroom with soothing green walls, a timbered ceiling, and soft rose carpet is reminiscent of a country cottage. The beautifully designed black iron bed evokes Victoriana and is covered with a comfy quilt. Floral curtains, framed prints, candles, and a foot warmer standing ready at the fireplace stove make perfect, decorative accessories.*

ABOVE: *This beautiful master bedroom combines all the requirements for comfort in a grand version of country Victorian style. The handsome, ornately carved canopy bed is covered by a charming country quilt, and a spacious wardrobe against the far wall provides ample room for storage. Casual sisal matting on the floor is dressed up with an oriental area rug. A lovely dressing table takes advantage of the natural lighting and view at the window.*

OPPOSITE: *Old-world cottage charm suffuses this inviting bedroom. A handsome iron and brass bed needs little more than a lovely white spread for embellishment. Floor-length floral curtains add a delicate touch, and a ribbon-motif wallpaper border inspires the color choice for the overhead lampshade and the upholstery on a button-tufted easy chair.*

CHAPTER FIVE

SPIRITED KITCHENS AND BATHS

No two rooms in the house are as hardworking as the kitchen and the bath. During the nineteenth century, the kitchen was the site of numerous household chores as well as culinary pursuits. The indoor bath, a true Victorian invention, became a necessity no home could do without—a welcome comfort in a modernizing world.

While the urban Victorian kitchen was often considered the domain of domestic servants, the rural or country kitchen was a warm, homey spot where the mistress of the house did her own cooking and the family often gathered for meals by the inviting warmth of the cookstove. Decoration in such a utilitarian space was given little thought throughout the nineteenth century and yet the kitchen acquired a charm all its own. Massive glass-front pantry cupboards; freestanding painted cupboards; gleaming metal stoves; tile, brick, or wood floors; and crisp, painted walls combined to create a room both practical and beautiful.

Today's country Victorian kitchen takes its cue from the best of the past. Consider cherry, oak, or pine cabinets with moldings and/or knobs to lend subtle architectural interest or opt for painted cabinetry that blends with the room's decor. A freestanding hutch, baker's cupboard, or piesafe will add nostalgic charm.

In decorating your kitchen, look to natural materials to evoke the spirit of country—ceramic tile floors and countertops, brick or wide-plank wood flooring, marble counters, and so on.

Beadboard wainscoting is ideal in the country Victorian kitchen. To achieve classic appeal, whitewash walls to play up a wood-beam or pressed-tin ceiling. Durable wallpaper is created today in myriad styles and patterns appropriate for the kitchen or bath. A stylized floral motif or miniprint are the perfect addition to either setting and contribute a welcome dose of Victoriana.

Brass lighting fixtures, overhead or fixed to the wall; a casual window treatment such as fabric shades or café curtains; and kitchen collectibles on display (vintage tea tins, enameled ware, yellow ware bowls, baskets, or copper cookware) are perfect finishing

OPPOSITE: *This kitchen corner is fully equipped to handle all tasks and playfully outfitted to reflect country Victorian spirit. An old-fashioned sink sports a green gingham skirt. A collection of enameled pots stacked by the stove, as well as the old advertising sign above the window, enhances the blue and white decor. Open shelves provide space for dishware and spices while window ledges are ideal for small plants and colored glass bottles and jars. The overhead rack keeps additional cookware handy, proving small spaces can be utilized to full advantage. Country colors and Victorian accessories certainly do go a long way in creating impressive style.*

touches. Shop the antiques shows and flea markets for these relics of the past and don't overlook the abundance of old dishware available to help set a casual kitchen table.

The country Victorian bath can likewise make use of old-time objects (or modern-day renditions). Brass, porcelain, and wood fixtures and hardware are right at home in this hardworking space. A ceramic tile floor in a checked pattern, or with an attractive floral motif, is the perfect backdrop for a refurbished or reproduction claw-foot tub and pedestal sink. Even an old case piece, such as a nineteenth-century washstand, can be adapted for use as a vanity.

Color, of course, is a matter of personal choice. In the country Victorian bath you can inject a bit of romanticism with pastels or create a more vibrant look with a stand-out green, blue, yellow, or red. Striking results can be achieved when walls are painted white and the trim treated to a deep shade of an accent color. Fresh flowers, herbs growing in clay pots, or a lush fern on a windowsill are all at home in country Victorian kitchens and baths.

ABOVE: *During the Victorian era before full rooms were dedicated to use as bathrooms, a bedroom was often used to accommodate indoor plumbing. Perhaps such was the case with this spacious bath. High ceilings and deep-set windows add architectural grandeur while opulent draperies contribute a touch of class. An antique metal tub is joined by an old-fashioned porcelain sink and simple furnishings that hint at a more casual, country style. Accessories are deliberately kept to a minimum to achieve the perfect effect.*

OPPOSITE: *This lovely room has it all: a handsome and fitting backdrop, a lavish window treatment with draperies puddling at the floor, a needlepoint rug for comfort and beauty underfoot, and a glorious old tub equipped with a shower. A handsome full-length mirror outfits a corner of the room while a small marble-top table resides in front of the window— elegant in a simple, charming way.*

OPPOSITE: *The beauty of natural wood tones is apparent in this casual kitchen where modern amenities blend comfortably with old-fashioned details. Built-in cabinets complement a scrubbed-top table and a sizable hutch filled with a collection of colorful dishware. Fresh flowers add a dose of Victorian charm.*

RIGHT, TOP: *Creating country Victorian ambience in the kitchen can often be accomplished by inviting one spectacular piece of furniture into the setting. Here, a beautifully painted step-back cupboard becomes an instant focal point. The open shelves are ideal for display, while cupboards below provide storage. By accessorizing this piece with a collection of dishware, cups, a green enameled ware bread box, a vintage scale, and a selection of wooden cutting boards, the owners have fashioned a perfect blend of country and Victorian kitchenware.*

RIGHT, BOTTOM: *Reminiscent of a nineteenth-century kitchen where glass-front cabinetry was used for storage, this functional and attractive space makes use of a handsome freestanding cupboard and open shelves to stock everyday pottery. A wood floor and butcher-block counter add notable country charm, and a floral tablecloth contributes a delicate touch of Victoriana. A collection of plates and prints on the earth-tone walls further enhance the decor.*

LEFT: *A blue and white color scheme sets the tone in this pleasing but cluttered kitchen. Victorian kitchen collectibles are displayed on countertops and in the blue hutch at the right while country-striped curtains and a checkered tablecloth add a playful touch. Dried flowers help bring the outdoors inside, as do the red poppies on the table. A storage bin situated against the wall on the right has been playfully embellished with paint to achieve the appearance of a miniature house.*

RIGHT: *Cottage ambience is clearly conveyed in this homey kitchen. A stone wall and timbered ceiling add a rustic touch while the scrubbed-top table and old-fashioned sink are reminiscent of nineteenth-century style. Bold, checkered curtains, an enameled ware bread box, and kitchen collectibles hung from wood beams are decorative country touches. The antique spinning wheel evokes a feeling of Victoriana.*

ABOVE: *Vivid color, a handsome crown molding at the ceiling, and an ornate chandelier bring a touch of elegance to this spacious, old-world kitchen. A scrubbed-top table is accompanied by a mix of slat-back chairs painted white. Necessary items as well as collectibles are casually displayed. Hand-painted floral motifs decorate the door and further brighten the lively space.*

LEFT, TOP: *The Victorians discovered that tile was not only practical; it was beautiful. Many china works factories operating in England and throughout Europe during the nineteenth century turned out exquisite examples. Here, a collection of antique tiles have been creatively arranged behind a sink to serve as a backsplash. This setting also showcases a collection of teapots atop a shelf. Mugs are kept handy on hooks.*

LEFT, BOTTOM: *Subtle decorative touches combine to create a warm, inviting space for this kitchen. A European-style sink is accessorized with gleaming brass taps, and artistic ceramic tiles make up the backsplash—a typically Victorian technique. To add a dash of "country," a window ledge showcases prized pottery and a rugged hanging shelf supports bottles, jars, and cooking implements. Windows with a view are treated to a pretty valance. The wood-beam ceiling contributes a hint of rustic charm.*

OPPOSITE: *These Victorian-inspired cupboards take architectural embellishment to new heights and set the tone in this beautiful kitchen. A vaulted ceiling adds spacious grandeur and the blue backdrop complements the warm wood tones. The ornate cabinetry is joined by a simple harvest table and slat-back chairs that infuse the setting with country charm.*

OPPOSITE: *In this bathroom, elements of both country and Victorian are combined harmoniously. A white beadboard wainscot and old-fashioned tub along with framed botanical prints comprise the Victorian aspect while a lace-edged shower curtain, yellow-painted walls, and a rustic wooden chair are indicative of country style.*

RIGHT: *Simple and lovely, this handsome bath recalls the nineteenth century via fixtures and beadboard wainscoting. A wall-hung porcelain sink is outfitted with a vintage mirror complete with towel bar and shelf for toiletries. In addition, Victorian-style hooks hold towels and matching wall sconces with frosted glass globes provide lighting. A plain wooden floor speaks of country charm, and the heat radiator—a household necessity—recalls the Victorians penchant for decorating even the most humble household object.*

ABOVE: *This upscale bath combines a beautiful backdrop and period-perfect "furnishings" with a wonderful collection of accessories. Soft green tiles inspire a matching window shade and the creative application of a wallpaper border adds subtle architectural interest. A claw-foot tub instantly conveys nineteenth-century spirit and is complemented by the ornately decorated mirror and sink. Spacious quarters allow for the addition of a comfortable easy chair and a tub-side table complete with a touch of greenery. A Victorian wall pocket is hung above the tub for a small bouquet of flowers.*

ABOVE: *This well-appointed room shows the bath can indeed be beautiful. The use of dark woods adds an elegant touch, as does the mirror above the sink—actually an over-mantel piece. It is a splendid example of giving new life to an architectural artifact. A Victorian folding screen is beautifully dressed in a patterned fabric that echoes the shades in the wallpaper, and plush towels are layered on a handsome rack. Decorative touches include simple portraits, a lovely bouquet of tulips, and eye-catching wall sconces that play up the glory of the gilded age.*

A B O V E : *Modern-day country Victorian decorating goes creative with this spectacular vanity. Custom-crafted with a beadboard wainscot, this curved unit becomes the focal point in this charming bath. An old-fashioned tub and floral wallpaper have been added for good measure. As a fine and fitting last touch, the ceiling has been papered to accent this spirited style.*

LEFT: *Four tiles bedecked with floral sprays serve as a backsplash for a beautiful china sink with a matching design. Plain white tiles are used in the tub area and help to tone down the red patterned wallpaper and floral wallpaper border. In truly romantic country Victorian style, accessories add to the romantic appeal—the china towel holder, the toothbrush and cup holder, and the attractive mirror with an ornate ribbon design.*

RIGHT: *Lovely details make this room special. The Victorian penchant for decoration is evident in the tiled and papered wall and the elaborate fringed and tasseled lampshade. The Victorian-style sink has an attractiveness all its own and recalls the simplified lines and crisp style so popular during the late 1800s. The wooden towel rack and old steamer trunk evoke the simple charms long associated with country style. The best of both decorating worlds has come together in this fine setting.*